I Count for Something

Written by: Phyllis Felicia
Illustrated by: Rebecca Bastian

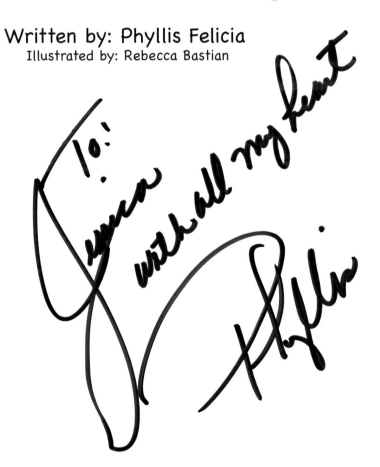

This book is dedicated to every child; you mean the world to us.
Kisses to the special little people who count for so many things in
"My Life": Anaiah, Jeric-Christian, Anna, Jacob and
the Clark & Claude Family.
Love,
Aunt Phyllis

I have one year to be one age.

I count for something.

1 (One) Year

2 (Two) Body Parts

I have two ears,
two eyes, two hands and two feet.

I count for something.

I have three reasons to smile;
for me, myself and I.

I count for something.

3 (Three) Pronouns

SUMMER

FALL

SPRING

WINTER

4 (Four) Seasons

I have four seasons to play in:
Summer to play in the sun,
Winter to build a snowman in the snow,
Fall to watch the leaves fall and
Spring to see the leaves grow.

I count for something.

5 (Five)Senses

I have five senses;
one to smell mommy's cookies,
two to touch her pretty face,
three to see daddy smile,
four to taste my birthday cake and
five to hear every one say they love me.

I Count for Something.

I have six vowels to learn
so I can read and write:
a, e, i, o, u and sometimes the letter y.

I count for something.

6 (Six) Vowels

I have seven days in the week
to visit 7 continents and cross 7 seas.
Sunday I'm in North America.
Monday I'm in Europe.
Tuesday I'm in Africa.
Wednesday I'm in Asia.
Thursday I'm in South America.
Friday its Australia,
and Saturday I'm in Antarctica,
preparing to do it all over again.

I count for something.

7 (Seven) Continents

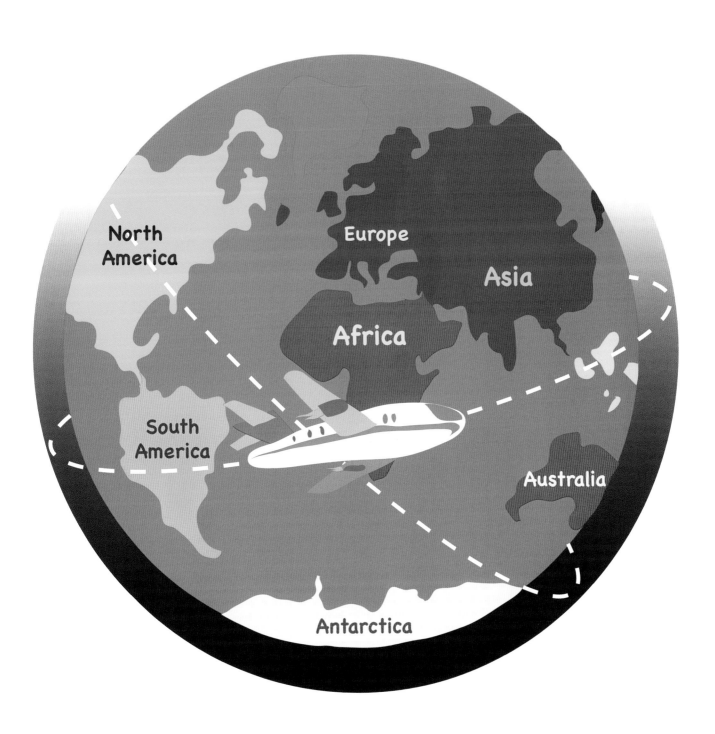

I have eight hours to go to school
and learn something new.
I also have eight crayons
in my coloring box:
red, black, orange, green,
yellow, purple, brown and blue.

I count for something.

8 (Eight) Colors

9 (Nine) Planets

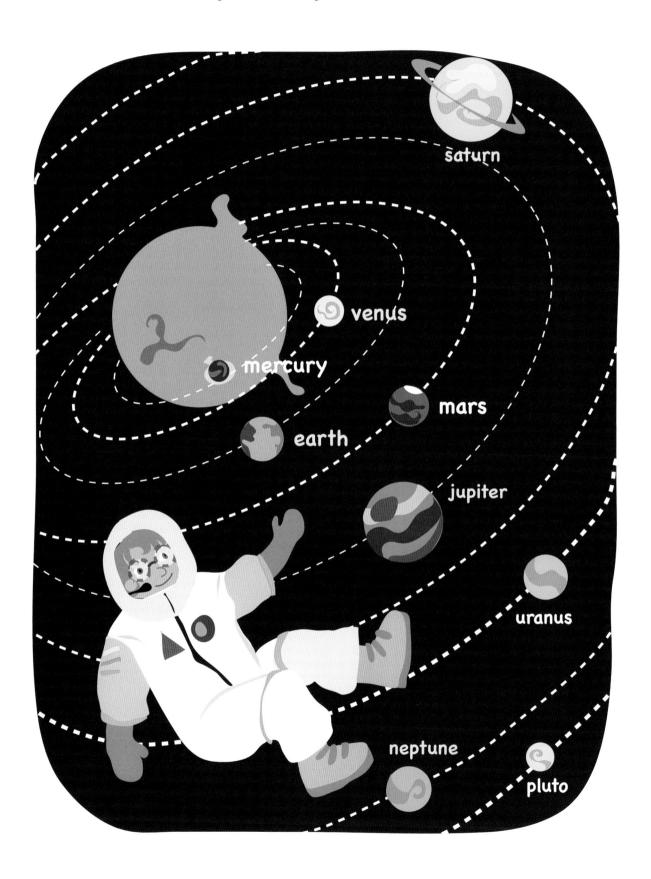

I had nine planets
to study in the solar system
until they undeclared one.
Yet, they all still look amazing
rotating around the sun...
Mercury, Venus, Earth, Mars,
Jupiter, Saturn, Uranus, Neptune,
and good old Pluto the ninth planet
declared a star.

I count for something.

I have ten fingers to grip a ball
and ten toes to balance me when I go.
I also have ten pennies in a dime
and 10 years to equal a decade in time.

I count for something.

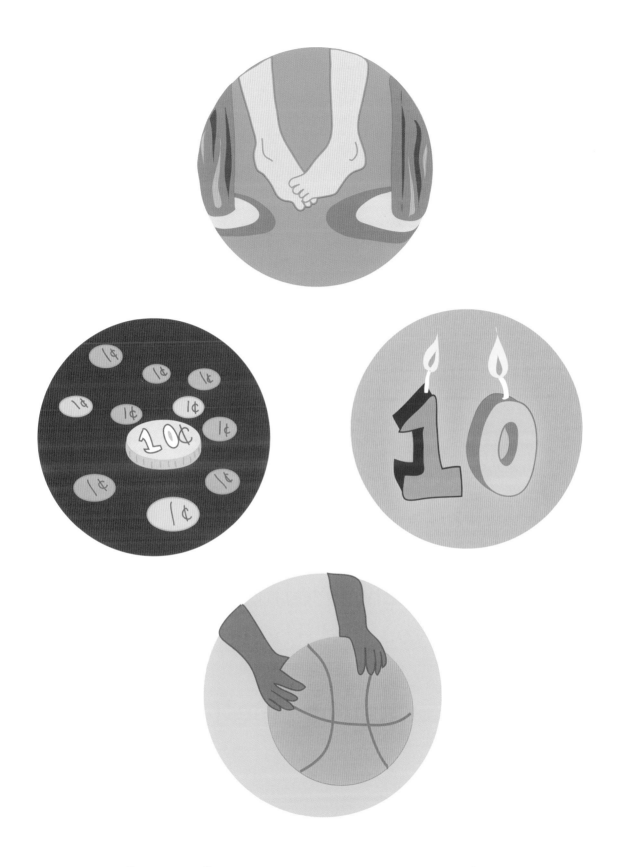

10 (Ten) Fingers and Toes

I have eleven different ways
to say thank you
when some one does something nice;

Wado, Merci,
Gracias, Toda,
Danke, Asante, Mahalo,

Do jeh, Gratias ago,
Thank you and Thoinks,moite!

I count for something.

11 (Eleven) Languages

I have twelve months and 365 days
to celebrate a dozen things in my life.
Each day of the month
I rise up early in the morning
to watch the stars go out of sight:
January, February, March,
April, May, June,
July, August, September, October,
November and December.

I count for something.

12 (Twelve) Months

Language Glossary

Wado-(Cherokee)
Merci-(French)
Gracias-(Spanish)
Toda-(Hebrew)
Danke-(German)
Thoinks, moite!-(Australian)
Asante-(Swahili)
Do jeh-(Chinese)
Gratias ago-(Latin)
Mahalo-(Hawaiian)
Thank you-(English)